TUDOR	STUART	GEORGIAN	VICTORIAN	MODERN TIMES
1485–1603	1603–1714	1714–1837	1837–1901	1902–NOW

children's HISTORY of LEEDS

Written by
Gillian Rogerson

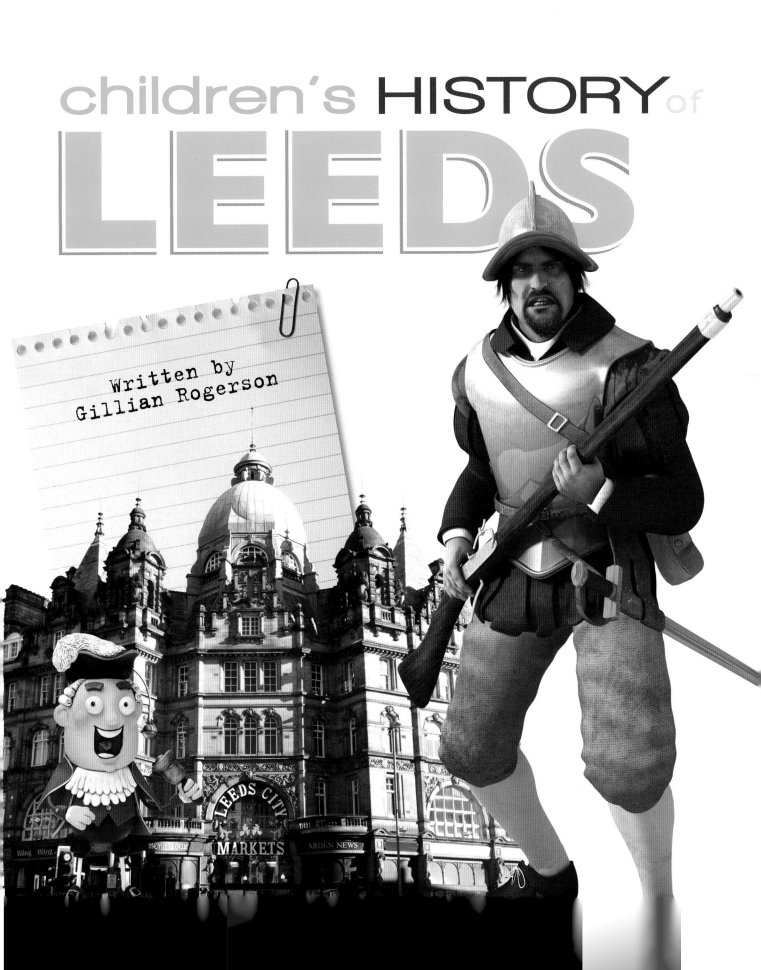

How well do you know your town?

Have you ever wondered what it would have been like living in Leeds when the Romans arrived? What about working at the mill instead of going to school? This book will uncover the important and exciting things that happened in your town.

Want to hear the other good bits? You will love this book! Some rather brainy folk have worked on it to make sure it's fun and informative. So what are you waiting for? Peel back the pages and be amazed at what happened in your town.

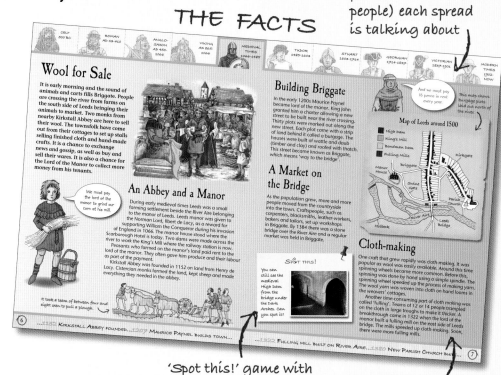

THE FACTS

Timeline shows which period (dates and people) each spread is talking about

'Spot this!' game with hints on something to find in your town

Clear informative text

THE EVIDENCE

Go back in time to read what it was like for children growing up in Leeds

Intriguing old photos

Hometown facts to amaze you!

Each period in the book ends with a summary explaining how we know about the past

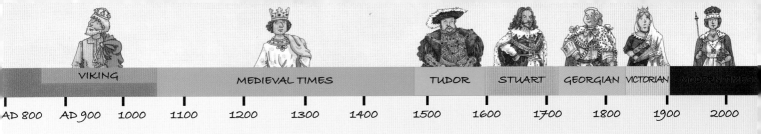

Contents

CELT
500 BC

ROMAN
AD 43-410

ANGLO-
SAXON
AD 450-
1066

VIKING
AD 865-
1066

MEDIEVA
TIMES
1066-
1485

A River-crossing

The Brigantes woman walks along the river carrying a heavy pot. She pulls her cloak tighter as the cold wind blows. She stops at the river crossing to watch the Roman soldiers making their way back to Adel. Not far now, she thinks. She is on her way to the market to sell her honey. The Romans at Adel have gold coins to spend. If she can sell her honey, she will buy a smooth Roman pot. They are lighter and easier to clean than the coil pots that the Brigantes make by hand.

We're the Brigantes – a Celtic tribe. We were here first!

SPOT THIS!

Can you spot the Roman stone coffin at Adel Church?

Romans in Adel

Before the Romans invaded West Yorkshire, the area was occupied by the Celtic Brigantes tribe, ruled over by Queen Cartimandua. In AD 155 a Brigantes revolt was put down by the Romans who had forts at Ilkley and Tadcaster. At that time, the area we call Leeds was covered in forest, with small farmsteads on the hills above the river. The River Aire was deep enough for boats to use. A Roman road crossed the River Aire near Castleford on the way to York. Romans may have settled around Leeds because pieces of Roman pottery and coins have been found. There is stronger evidence that they built a fort and settlement at Adel, 8 kilometres to the north of Leeds.

Loidis to Ledes

The history of Leeds itself really begins after the Romans left in AD 410. The Anglo-Saxons, who had been raiding Britain from across the North Sea, began to settle alongside the local people. A raised bank, known as Grim's Ditch, to the east of Leeds at Temple Newsam, may have been a defence against the invading Romans and, later, the Anglo-Saxons.

You can see this Anglo-Saxon stone cross at Leeds Parish Church. There are fragments of other crosses in Leeds City Museum.

People who were born in Leeds are known as 'Loiners'.

This carved Viking bodkin made from walrus tusk is in Leeds City Museum.

In Anglo-Saxon times, the area we call Leeds was part of Elmet Forest.

How do we know?

In AD 731 a monk called Bede wrote The Ecclesiastical History of The English People. He told of an old town with a church which had been destroyed by fire. But new dwellings were built there by later kings. Bede called this place 'Loidis'. Over three hundred years later, the Domesday Book records a number of buildings and a parish church in a place called 'Ledes'.

In 1702, a Leeds historian, Ralph Thoresby, recorded in his diary that two cartloads of Roman remains had been unearthed at nearby Adel. He found tombstones, pottery and coins.

In 1838 the remains of stone crosses were found when Leeds Parish Church tower was demolished. The crosses, from the 9th and 10th centuries, tell us that although Leeds was a small settlement it attracted people who could afford marked graves.

CELT
500 BC

ROMAN
AD 43-410

ANGLO-
SAXON
AD 450-
1066

VIKING
AD 865-
1066

MEDIEVA
TIMES
1066-148

Wool for Sale

It is early morning and the sound of animals and carts fills Briggate. People are crossing the river from farms on the south side of Leeds bringing their animals to market. Two monks from nearby Kirkstall Abbey are here to sell their wool. The townsfolk have come out from their cottages to set up stalls selling finished cloth and hand-made crafts. It is a chance to exchange news and gossip, as well as buy and sell their wares. It is also a chance for the Lord of the Manor to collect more money from his tenants.

We must pay the lord of the manor to grind our corn at his mill.

An Abbey and a Manor

During early medieval times Leeds was a small farming settlement beside the River Aire belonging to the manor of Leeds. Leeds manor was given to the Norman lord, Ilbert de Lacy, as a reward for supporting William the Conqueror during his invasion of England in 1066. The manor house stood where the Scarborough Hotel is today. Two dams were made across the river to work the King's Mill where the railway station is now.

Peasants who farmed on the manor's land paid rent to the lord of the manor. They often gave him produce and their labour as part of the payment.

Kirkstall Abbey was founded in 1152 on land from Henry de Lacy. Cistercian monks farmed the land, kept sheep and made everything they needed in the abbey.

It took a team of between four and eight oxen to pull a plough.

...1152 KIRKSTALL ABBEY FOUNDED...1207 MAURICE PAYNEL BUILDS TOWN...

TUDOR 1485-1603	STUART 1603-1714	GEORGIAN 1714-1837	VICTORIAN 1837-1901	MODERN TIMES 1902-NOW

Building Briggate

In the early 1200s, Maurice Paynel became lord of the manor. King John granted him a charter allowing a new street to be built near the river crossing. Thirty plots were marked out along the new street. Each plot came with a strip of land behind it called a burgage. The houses were built of wattle and daub (timber and clay) and roofed with thatch. This street became known as Briggate, which means 'way to the bridge'.

A Market on the Bridge

As the population grew, more and more people moved from the countryside into the town. Craftspeople, such as carpenters, blacksmiths, leather-workers, bakers and tailors, set up workshops in Briggate. By 1384 there was a stone bridge over the River Aire and a regular market was held in Briggate.

And we must pay 16 pence in rent every year.

This map shows burgage plots laid out north of the river.

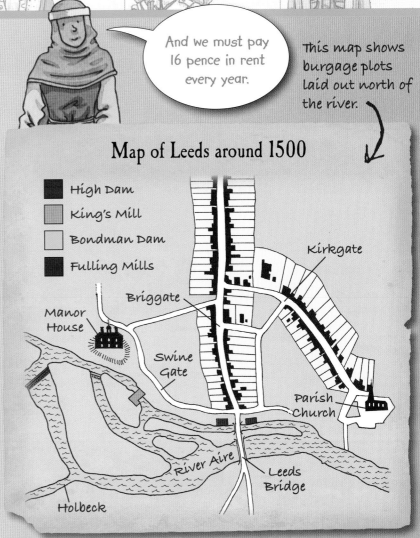

Map of Leeds around 1500

High Dam · King's Mill · Bondman Dam · Fulling Mills

Kirkgate · Briggate · Manor House · Swine Gate · Parish Church · River Aire · Leeds Bridge · Holbeck

SPOT THIS!

You can still see the medieval High Dam from the bridge under the Dark Arches. Can you spot it?

Cloth-making

One craft that grew rapidly was cloth-making. It was popular as wool was easily available. Around this time spinning wheels became more common. Before this, spinning was done by hand using a simple spindle. The spinning wheel speeded up the process of making yarn. The wool yarn was woven into cloth on hand looms in the weavers' cottages.

Another time-consuming part of cloth-making was called 'fulling'. Teams of 12 or 14 people trampled on the cloth in large troughs to make it thicker. A breakthrough came in 1322 when the lord of the manor built a fulling mill on the east side of Leeds bridge. The mill speeded up cloth-making. Soon, there were more fulling mills.

CELT
500 BC

ROMAN
AD 43-410

ANGLO-
SAXON
AD 450-
1066

VIKING
AD 865-
1066

MEDIEVA
TIMES
1066-148

When the market grew in Briggate, some farmers decided to leave their fields and make a living from crafts. Here is an imaginary account from Ruth, a 10-year-old girl who is moving from her home on the farm to Briggate.

My job is to spin the wool into yarn. I also feed the pigs and hens, and fetch the water from the river.

Monday, 3rd May, 1400

I didn't want to leave our farm, I liked living there. But it rained and rained last summer and we couldn't harvest the crops. They just lay rotting in the field. Father said we could either starve or move. So here we are in Briggate on the other side of the river. I didn't like it at first. It was too crowded and too noisy. The house is made of wood and not stone like our cosy farmhouse. Father told me we'd have to earn our keep spinning wool. I told him he could spin if he wanted to but I was going back to the farm. Then Mother told me that we'd have a new spinning wheel – not just a spindle to spin on. She is teaching me how to use it. It was a bit tricky at first but I soon got used to it. The best part is that Father says we're going to buy a loom to weave our own cloth next. Then we can sell the cloth we make right outside our front door on market day! I really like living in Briggate now – it's so much livelier than the farm.

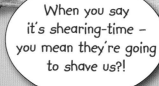

When you say it's shearing-time – you mean they're going to shave us?!

Wet cloth was hung out to dry on wooden frames called tenterhooks. Can you see the tenterhooks down by the river?

TUDOR
1485-1603

STUART
1603-1714

GEORGIAN
1714-1837

VICTORIAN
1837-1901

MODERN
TIMES
1902-
NOW

A medieval tomb in Leeds Parish Church.

Briggate means 'way to the bridge'. Kirkgate means 'way to the church'.

How do we know?

When William the Conqueror's Norman officials came to Leeds they recorded what they saw in the Domesday Book, written in 1086. It tells us that Leeds had twenty-seven farm-workers, four small-holders, four freemen, fourteen ploughs, a priest, a church, a mill and ten acres of meadow.

We know how Leeds developed during medieval times because written records of payments to the lord of the manor have survived. A document dated 1185 tells us that the Lord of Leeds Manor, Ilbert de Lacy, also owned two mills at Temple Newsam, east of Leeds: one for grinding corn and one for fulling cloth.

In 1207 a monk named Serlo wrote down from memory how Kirkstall Abbey was built over 50 years earlier.

Looking at maps is one of the best ways to get an idea of how a city has changed over time. The first surviving map of Leeds was drawn in 1560. It shows clearly how the plots of land in Kirkgate and Briggate were marked out.

From an abbey and a manor, Leeds quickly grew into a bustling, wealthy market town.

Set into the wall of the Parish Church on Kirkgate, the East Bar stone marks the eastern boundary of medieval Leeds.

CELT
500 BC

ROMAN
AD 43-410

ANGLO-
SAXON
AD 450-
1066

VIKING
AD 865-
1066

MEDIEVAL
TIMES
1066-
1485

Bustling Briggate

The boy hurries through the back streets. He is late for school and has a long walk ahead of him. In a backyard, he passes a young girl at a water trough washing grease and dirt from a smelly pile of fleeces. Through the open door behind her, he sees her mother feed wool through the spinning wheel. Next door, a man checks the cloth being woven on a handloom. How different his life is from theirs, he thinks. Perhaps lessons in Latin and Greek are not so hard after all.

When Red Hall, built in 1628, was finally demolished a cannon ball from the Civil War was found buried in a wall.

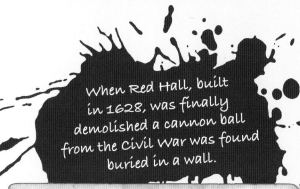

On 22nd November, 1539, Abbot Ripley surrendered Kirkstall Abbey to Richard Layton, one of Henry VIII's men.

Henry VIII

When Henry VIII sent his men to close Kirkstall Abbey in 1539, a prosperous community was lost forever. Reverend William Sheafield left money in his will to set up a new grammar school for Leeds which opened in 1552. Later, in 1624, a wealthy cloth merchant called John Harrison provided a new building for the grammar school as well as almshouses for the poor.

Wealthy merchants built grand houses on the edge of the town in Boar Lane and Town End. The merchants began to have more say in the running of the town. The lord of the manor was no longer in charge. By 1600, 3,000 people – half the population of Leeds – were crammed into Briggate and Kirkgate. New homes were built in yards, orchards, gardens and any other space available.

Mayor and Corporation

In 1626 the king, Charles I, made Leeds a 'free borough'. This gave the town local powers to govern itself. The Corporation Seal of 1626 was used to stamp or seal important legal documents. Sir John Savile was the first alderman (mayor) of Leeds.

Civil War

The Civil War came to Leeds in 1643. The town supported the king, Charles I, against Parliament. Sir William Savile gathered together Royalist troops to fight against Parliament's Roundhead army. A two-metre trench was dug from St John's Church to the Upper Headrow. On 23rd January, 1643, Sir Thomas Fairfax led his troops towards Leeds. Fairfax had many more men than Savile. A battle developed on all sides of Leeds which spread into Briggate and Boar Lane. Fairfax soon overpowered Savile. Five hundred prisoners were taken but Fairfax let them go on the promise that they wouldn't take up arms again against Parliament.

Leeds coat of arms shows a fleece and three owls. The fleece shows the importance of wool. The owls were part of the coat of arms of Sir John Savile.

King Charles I was held prisoner in the Red Hall in 1647.

Cloth Halls

During the 1600s cloth-making boomed. Spinning and weaving took place in cottages in Leeds and the surrounding areas. The finished cloth was sold to merchants at the market held in Briggate on Tuesdays and Saturdays. By this time, Leeds merchants were selling their cloth abroad. So they put a lot of money into the building of the Aire and Calder Navigation Canal. This was completed in 1699 linking Leeds with the coastal ports.

In 1711 the first indoor cloth market was built – the White Cloth Hall in Kirkgate. This allowed people to trade in comfort. More cloth halls soon followed.

Chew this. It might not work but it'll help take your mind off the scabs.

SPOT THIS!

Can you spot the dome on the top of the White Cloth Hall?

Plague swept through Leeds in 1645 killing 1,300 people in 9 months. The market remained open but people had to produce a medical certificate to prove they didn't have the plague.

This is an imaginary account of 10-year-old John whose father is a wealthy cloth merchant. John goes to Leeds Grammar school where he learns Latin and Greek. On market days he helps his father to haggle with the rich foreign merchants who come to Leeds market to buy cloth.

> Our school motto is 'Nullius Non Mater Disciplinae'. It means 'Nothing if not the Mother of Learning'.

Monday, 5th April, 1680

It was market day today, so I didn't go to school. Father wanted me to go with him to help bargain with the foreign cloth-buyers. On the way there, Father reminded me to speak very quietly when the market opened and only speak when he asked me to. When we got to Briggate there was nobody else there. Then at 7 o'clock the bell sounded and lots of people came rushing from the public houses. We quickly set up our trestle table and laid out the cloth. A few minutes later some richly dressed merchants walked up and down the rows of tables looking at the cloth. One man stopped at our table. He nodded and Father pointed to me. The man leaned over and whispered. I told Father what he said and Father told me what to whisper back. We whispered back and forth until they had agreed a price. Then they nodded at each other and Father rolled up a bolt of cloth and gave it to the man's servant. The man gave Father gold coins from his purse. Now I am almost nodding off, but still have homework to finish before my candle burns down.

Leeds Grammar School was in Headingley Lane between 1579 and 1624.

Did you Know that the gatehouse of Kirkstall Abbey is now part of Abbey House Museum?

This is how Leeds looked from the south side of the River Aire in the 1600s.

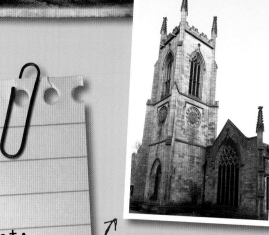

Leeds had a White Cloth Hall for trading undyed cloth and a Coloured Cloth Hall for trading dyed cloth.

St John the Evangelist Church, built in 1634, is the oldest in Leeds.

How do we know?

Daniel Defoe, who wrote Robinson Crusoe, visited Leeds in 1724. He described how business was conducted in the cloth market:

'Before the market bell rings, no man shews a piece of cloth, nor can the clothiers sell any but in open market. After the market bell rings again, no body stays a moment in the market, but carries his cloth back if it be not sold. And that which is most admirable is, 'tis all managed with the most profound silence, and you cannot hear a word spoken in the whole market, I mean, by the persons buying and selling; 'tis all done in whisper.'

Old parish churches kept a register of births, marriages and deaths going back to Tudor times. Leeds parish register records the burial of the first plague victim in March 1645: 'Alice, wife of John Musgrave, of Vicar Laine'. It also records the deaths of soldiers in the Civil War: 'A souldier, a grey coat under Marquesse of Newcastle' and 'A souldier for the Parliament'.

War, plague and religion made Leeds a dangerous place to live in Tudor and Stuart times.

Smoke and Dust

The little girl crawls quickly under the machine. The huge shuttles whizz past her ears. The smell of hot oil makes her eyes water. She reaches out her aching arm and grabs a handful of fluff. She crawls back out. No injuries – this time. She is so sleepy after working for ten hours. But she has to stay awake – if she falls asleep, she might be beaten.

Benjamin Gott became mayor of Leeds in 1799.

A New Kind of Mill

Up until now, the merchants of Leeds bought their finished cloth from clothiers who made it in their homes. But one merchant, called Benjamin Gott, decided to bring the whole manufacturing process together in one place. In 1782 he built a mill on the western edge of Leeds. The mill was extremely successful and produced huge amounts of cloth quickly. Within 10 years Gott had built mills in Armley and Burley. By 1797 he employed 1,200 workers. Gott's cloth was sold around the world, even supplying blankets and uniforms for the English army fighting in France.

The mills were powered by water from the River Aire. The finished cloth was transported along the canals – the Aire and Calder Canal to the east and the Leeds and Liverpool canal, completed in 1816, to the west. The Middleton Railway arrived in Leeds in 1758, carrying coal to and from the heart of Leeds. It is the UK's oldest working railway.

Armley Mills was the largest wool mill in the world when it was built. It used the latest steam-powered looms. Today it is a museum.

...1770 LEEDS POTTERY ESTABLISHED...1782 GOTT BUILDS FIRST MILL...

Factory Work

By 1822 there were around 40 factories in Leeds. Skilled workers were no longer needed because new steam-powered machines could do their work more quickly and cheaply. Many cloth-making jobs disappeared.

Workers who had lost their jobs began protesting, attacking factories and breaking the new machines that had replaced them. During riots in 1812 and 1842 the Leeds authorities had to call in the military.

Working conditions in the factories were horrific. Women and children as young as six years old were employed to work in the mills because they were paid lower wages. The factories were hot and airless. The noisy machines didn't have any safety guards around them. People often worked 69 hours a week or more in these dangerous conditions, and might be hit with a strap to make them work faster.

The Aire and Calder Canal, undated.

Barges linked together and pulled along the Aire and Calder Canal were known as Tom Puddings.

The rioters were eventually rounded up and the leaders hanged!

Back-to-backs

The growing population of Leeds needed homes. Trees were cut down and meadows disappeared as the first back-to-back houses were built. These were rows of houses where the back of one house joined the back of another. Briggate became dirty and overcrowded. The air around Leeds became thick with smoke from the factories.

The unhealthy living conditions led to a cholera outbreak in 1832 which killed over 700 people. The crime rate increased and it wasn't long before the wealthy mill owners moved out of Leeds to the surrounding countryside of Chapel Allerton, Headingley and Potternewton.

After 1790, scavengers collected the night's sewage on soilcarts. Lucky me!

SPOT THIS!

Can you spot this canal marker stone which gives the distance between Leeds and Liverpool?

LPOOL 127 MILES

Once the factories arrived, people could no longer make a living spinning and weaving at home. Here is an imaginary conversation between 10-year-old Alice, who works as a scavenger at the mill keeping the machinery clear of bits of cotton and fluff, and Tom, a barge boy who lives and works on the canal. He delivers raw cotton to the mill and picks up finished cloth to take to Liverpool.

My ma says we're lucky to have the work and not be in the workhouse.

Friday, 25th September, 1825

Tom: My family lives on the canal, so I've always worked on the barges. I like the outdoor life, though it's bitter in winter.

Alice: I've worked at the mill since I was seven years old. I have to get here by 6 o'clock in the morning. Sometimes I'm late because we don't have a clock at home. If I'm late I get hit with the strap.

Tom: I'm always up with the lark or my da' would be after me. My ma gets us porridge for breakfast.

Alice: I don't get a proper break at work and often eat my oatcake standing up. The food gets covered in fluff so I have to pick that off before I can eat it.

Tom: Sometimes we walk through the night to get our load delivered. It's 127 miles to Liverpool (200 km).

Alice: Work finishes at about 9 o'clock at night. My friend told me that the owner sometimes lies about the time and makes us work until 11 o'clock. I'm always tired at the end of the day. There are often accidents at work. When I first started at the mill I wasn't quick enough when I crawled under the machines. My hair got caught and a big chunk was pulled out. It was awful.

Tom: My brother fell in the canal and was drowned – you see, he couldn't swim.

1833 Factory Reform Act

- Children aged under 9 must not work in the textile mills.
- Children aged 9-13 must not work more than 8 hours, with an hour's break for lunch.
- Children aged 9-13 must have 2 hours of education a day.
- Children aged 14-18 years must not work more than 12 hours a day, with an hour's break for lunch.
- Children aged under 18 must not work at night.

The Sadler Report led to the 1833 Factory Reform Act which gave working children better protection. But there were very few inspectors to enforce the law.

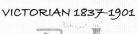

Life was very different for the merchants and mill owners. They attended grand balls and concerts at the Assembly Rooms.

I've lost a fortune gambling at the Assembly Rooms.

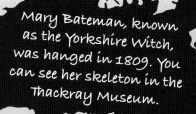

Mary Bateman, known as the Yorkshire Witch, was hanged in 1809. You can see her skeleton in the Thackray Museum.

A creamware chocolate kettle made at Leeds Pottery.

Leeds' factories made their owners very rich, but left some workers very poor.

How do we know?

By Georgian times, there were plenty of written records, including newspapers like the *Leeds Mercury* established in 1718, and the *Leeds Intelligence*, published in 1754. The *Leeds Directory* of 1798 tells us how many coaches left Leeds daily: five coaches set out from the Old King's Arms for London, Manchester, Sheffield, Hull and Newcastle; two left from the Golden Lion daily, for London and Manchester; three departed from the Rose and Crown, for Liverpool and Hull.

The 1832 Sadler Report, from the House of Commons, tells us about the working conditions and health of children from Leeds. When Michael Sadler moved to Leeds in 1800 he became increasingly concerned about the working conditions of children. He interviewed 89 child workers about their appalling conditions. Sir Samuel Smith, a doctor in Leeds, reported that, up to the age of 12, children's bones are soft and still developing. Long periods of standing caused severe damage, in particular a deformity known as 'knock-knees'.

A Railway Arrives

At 6:30 am a crowd of almost 20,000 people wait in the rain at Marsh Lane terminus. The first ever train on the Leeds to Selby Railway is about to leave. Despite the dreary weather, everyone is eager to witness the *Nelson* steam engine. By the time it returns to Leeds later that morning, the weather has improved and the crowd has grown to 40,000. A rumour quickly spreads that the *Nelson* reached a speed of 32 kph on the downhill run to Selby!

John Waddington started as a printer. His firm had become the world's biggest card and game manufacturer by the 1920s.

The new cast iron Leeds Bridge was opened in 1873 to cope with the increased traffic. Louis le Prince filmed the traffic in 1888, taking some of the first ever moving pictures.

Rapid Changes

Traffic on the Aire and Calder Canal became so heavy that it caused jams. Faster transport was needed. The Leeds to Selby Railway opened in 1834 followed, five years later, by the Leeds to Manchester Railway connecting Leeds with London. Rapid changes followed as transport improved.

The clothing industry grew. At the new Temple Mill, John Marshall kept sheep on a grass-covered roof which helped keep the building cool. The mill's success was helped by engineer Matthew Murray who improved the machine design. John Barran set up a factory in Boar Lane using the new Singer sewing machines to produce ready-made clothes. His massive warehouse, St Paul's House, is still in Park Square. Stead & Simpson employed over 1,000 people making around 7,000 pairs of boots a week.

Other industries grew too. Leeds became a centre for printing, especially when Alfred Cooke built the world's biggest printing works on Hunslet Road. Many Leeds firms and products became household names – Tetley's Bitter, Moorhouse's Jam and Goodall and Backhouse's 'Yorkshire Relish'.

TUDOR 1485-1603

STUART 1603-1714

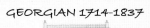
GEORGIAN 1714-1837

VICTORIAN 1837-1901

MODERN TIMES
1902-NOW

A New City

The city's success attracted people who set up new industries. Jewish and Irish immigrants came to Leeds to find work and escape worse conditions at home. By the end of the 19th century Leeds had grown into the fourth largest city in England.

Kirkgate Market was opened in 1857. A young Jewish immigrant, called Michael Marks, set up a Penny Bazaar there. He later went into partnership with Tom Spencer to form Marks & Spencer. New shopping arcades were built along Briggate. The Grand Theatre opened in 1878.

Leeds needed a new town hall. A competition to design it was won by Cuthbert Broderick. The new Town Hall was completed in 1858 and officially opened by Queen Victoria. This was a great day of celebration for Leeds and showed the rest of England how important Leeds was becoming.

The following year, the Yorkshire Penny Saving Bank (the Yorkshire Bank) opened. By the time the Bank of England opened, Leeds was an important financial centre. In 1893, Leeds officially became a city.

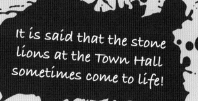
It is said that the stone lions at the Town Hall sometimes come to life!

The Corn Exchange, designed by Cuthbert Broderick (right), was built in 1864 for trading corn.

A picture of the new Leeds Town Hall appeared in The Illustrated London News on 11th September, 1858.

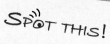
SPOT THIS!

Can you spot this clock in Thornton's Arcade? It has moving figures of Robin Hood, Friar Tuck, Richard the Lionheart and Gurth the Swineherd.

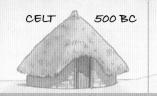 
Rich and Poor

It is still dark as people shuffle out of their homes. Their wooden clogs clatter on the cobbles, squelching through the mud and dirt on the streets. The air is thick with smoke. People cough constantly as they walk through the streets of back-to-back houses. Their tired feet carry them towards the factories.

The Bear Pit on Cardigan Road, Headingley, is all that's left of Leeds' Zoological and Botanical Gardens.

The air is so much fresher in the suburbs!

Slums...

Factory workers needed cheap housing quickly. The first back-to-back houses on Union Street, Ebenezer Street and George Street were built around the beginning of the 1800s. Back-to-back houses built in Hunslet and Armley were so close together that they didn't have much light or ventilation inside. There were no drains so waste was thrown out into the street. Any spare land which had not been built on was used as a dump for rubbish. Some people kept pigs or chickens in their yards. This added to the hygiene problems of the town centre. There was a shared 'privy' for people to use, but these were not emptied often.

...and Villas

Richer people moved further away to the new suburbs of Headingley, Potternewton, Adel and Roundhay. They built brick villas with space for live-in servants and gardens. These houses had better drains and people could pay for a clean water supply to the house.

Armley House in Gott's Park was the family home of mill-owner, Benjamin Gott.

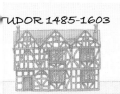 
Squalor and Cholera

As well as the squalid living conditions, workers had to put up with smoke pollution from the mills, factories, foundries, gasworks and brickyards. The smoke pollution was so bad that plants wouldn't grow. People suffered from ill health and the death rate rose. Leeds town centre became dirty and overcrowded. The River Aire became polluted with waste from the sewers and factories. Dead animals were thrown into the river along with household rubbish. Disease spread quickly. There was a further cholera outbreak in 1848 which killed 2,000 people.

Aire and Calder Navigation.
NOTICE

To Inspectors & Superintendents of the Aire and Calder Navigation; also to Captains of Dredgers and Fly Boats, and others.

DROWNED PERSONS
(DISCOVERY and INTERMENT) ACT, 1886

The above Act provides that any person finding a Dead Human Body in the Navigation, shall within six hours give notice of the finding of such dead human Body to a Police Constable, who will make the necessary arrangements for its removal and interment, and the Superintendent of the Police for the district in which such dead human body shall be found and brought to bank, will pay the person first giving such information the sum of **FIVE SHILLINGS**. Any person finding a Dead Human Body in the Navigation, and not giving notice as aforesaid, will be liable to a Penalty of **FIVE POUNDS**.

A notice from Aire and Calder Canal gives us an idea of how polluted the waterways were.

Leeds General Infirmary was opened by the Prince of Wales in 1868.

Medicine and Fresh Air

Towards the end of Victorian times, things began to improve in Leeds. The old Leeds General Infirmary was rebuilt with planning advice from Florence Nightingale. A 10-year-old boy from Dewsbury was the first person to be admitted to the new hospital in May 1869.

The City Council created parks to provide Leeds people with fresh air and exercise. Roundhay Park was bought in 1871. A year later, 100,000 people came to watch Prince Arthur officially open the park to the public.

SPOT THIS!

In 1891 an electric trolley bus service began between the city centre and Roundhay Park. Can you spot some of the old trolley poles in Roundhay car park?

Education

For the first time, children between the ages of five and 12 had to go to a national school or a church school. Some factory owners, like John Marshall, set up schools for their workers' children. He also helped set up the Mechanics' Institute. The first public libraries opened in the 1880s. Yorkshire College, opened in 1874, became Leeds University in 1905.

By Victorian times, three in every four houses in Leeds were back-to-back houses. Each house had one room upstairs and one downstairs. The back of one house joined the back of another. There were windows on one side of the house only. The downstairs room was used for living, washing and eating in, quite often it was also used as a bedroom. The upstairs room was used as a bedroom. Here is the imaginary diary entry of Rose, a 10-year-old factory girl who lived in such a house:

I hope I get a good night's sleep tonight! It's early Mass at church tomorrow.

Saturday, 11th September, 1852

I got up, as usual, at 5 o'clock this morning. My sister Elsie and I sleep downstairs so I always check for rats first. My sister made up the fire while I lit a candle. It's always dark in our house, even in the middle of summer. I'll skip having a wash until Sunday. It's my turn to empty our toilet bucket in the yard. I'm not using that stinky privy at the end of the street – it hasn't been emptied for months! The neighbours were so noisy last night I hardly slept a wink. Next door left were shouting and fighting (I think he drinks!). Behind us the new baby was wailing all hours of the night. And the boy next door right doesn't stop coughing. (The Irish woman over the street coughed so much that she died!) I made a pot of tea for my mum and dad and took it upstairs. Mum and Dad share a bed with my little sister and brother. Dad, me and Elsie set off for the factory at half past 5. We took our breakfast to eat at work. When we got home, Mum had put the little ones to bed. She'd cleaned the house this morning but by the time we came back from work it was covered in soot from the fire again. Poor Mum was too worn out to complain!

Leeds built more back-to-back houses and kept building them longer than any other town.

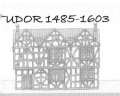

Leeds Union Workhouse is now the Thackray Museum.

St Anne's Cathedral was built to serve the growing number of Catholic Irish coming to live in Leeds.

Leeds Rhinos and Yorkshire County Cricket Club moved to their new home stadium at Headingley in 1890.

The population of Leeds rocketed from 30,669 in 1801 to 177,920 by 1901.

Joshua Tetley's Brewery workers became volunteers for the Leeds Rifles, formed in 1859.

How do we know?

The Victorians left diaries, documents and, for the first time, photographs of what life was like for both rich and poor people.

Dr Robert Baker was a Leeds surgeon who found a link between areas of disease and houses with poor drainage. In a report he wrote:

'The surface of these streets is considerably elevated by accumulated ashes and filth: privies so laden with ashes as to be unusable.'

In contrast, a newspaper report from March 1869 described the trains arriving in Leeds city centre:

'The sight of a locomotive steaming across some of the principal streets of Leeds was so entirely novel that the spectacle caused no small amount of amazement. The moving locomotive was best seen from Briggate. Passers-by in the leading thoroughfares gazed in wonderment and admiration, and trades people hastened to the doors of their business premises, only to join in the expression of astonishment.'

CELT
500 BC

ROMAN
AD 43-410

ANGLO-
SAXON
AD 450-
1066

VIKING
AD 865-
1066

MEDIEVAL
TIMES
1066-
1485

A New Century

The women change into their smocks, caps and rubber-soled shoes. They walk towards the shell workshop where they will spend the day filling shell-cases with explosives. As they pass the remains of Room 42 they all say a silent prayer for the people who had died last week. They also pray for their own safety.

Dangerous Times

When World War One broke out in 1914 guns and munitions were needed urgently. A munitions factory was quickly built between Crossgates and Garforth. Thousands of men had joined the armed services so most of the workers were women. They filled shells and cartridges with explosives. On 5th December, 1916 there was an explosion in Room 42. Thirty-five workers were killed and many injured. The public were not told about the accident until six years after the war ended.

In 1921, a Jewish refugee calling himself Montague Burton set up a clothing factory in Hudson Road. It became the largest in Europe.

IN MEMORY OF
THE BARNBOW SHELL FACTORY
WORKERS
WHO LOST THEIR LIVES DURING
THE
1914-18 WAR

Barnbow Factory is no longer there, but there is a memorial stone on the main road through Crossgates.

Barnbow girls drank lots of milk to stop their skin turning yellow from handling explosive powder called cordite.

Blackburn Aircraft Ltd in Leeds built the Skua – the first aircraft to sink a warship in wartime.

World War Two

During World War Two children from Leeds were evacuated from their homes to live in the countryside where they would be safe from bombing raids. Leeds was luckier than a lot of cities, suffering just nine bombing raids. The worst night of bombing was in March 1941 when 77 people were killed. Almost 200 buildings were damaged, including the Town Hall.

The small airport at Leeds Bradford became a testing ground for the new aircraft built at the Avro factory next door.

...1914-1918 WORLD WAR ONE...1935 LEEDS AND BRADFORD AIRPORT OPENS...

A New Beginning

By the 1970s much of the cloth-making industry had moved abroad where workers could be paid less. But Leeds kept its tailors, shoemakers and engineering firms.

Leeds Council started to demolish the back-to-backs. New council estates were built in Gipton, Meanwood, Crossgates, Middleton and York Road. Private houses were built in Alwoodley, Oakwood and Adel. More schools were built and the council took over the running of colleges. Leeds Council became one of the biggest employers in the city.

The Civic Hall in Millennium Square was opened in 1933.

Leeds Jamiah Mosque is part of an Islamic centre.

The first Leeds Asian Mela was held in 1996.

The Sikh Temple in Chapeltown is the largest in Leeds.

SPOT THIS!

Can you spot this statue of Arthur Louis Aaron? He became a hero in World War Two when his fighter plane was shot down. Although fatally injured, he and his crew landed the plane safely. He died nine hours later.

Newcomers

After the war, industries were beginning to grow again. There were not enough workers in Britain to fill all the jobs. During the 1950s people from the West Indies, India and Pakistan were encouraged by the British government to come to Leeds to live and work. They settled in Chapeltown and Harehills.

Not everyone welcomed the newcomers, but Leeds has benefited over the years with new restaurants, shops and places of worship. The West Indian Carnival was the first of its kind in Europe. Today, in most parts of the city, people live and work well together, celebrating a shared pride in being 'Loiners'.

CELT
500 BC

ROMAN
AD 43-410

ANGLO-
SAXON
AD 450-
1066

VIKING
AD 865-
1066

MEDIEVA
TIMES
1066-
1485

By the 1960s people from all over the world were living in Leeds. Here is an imaginary diary entry from a 10-year-old boy called Lester, whose father and mother came from the West Indies in the 1950s.

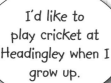

I'd like to play cricket at Headingley when I grow up.

Tuesday, 1st August, 1967

I'm hurrying to finish my homework before Dad gets home. He's on late shift on the buses, so he won't be home 'til later but he's been teaching me to play the steel pan and he said he'd take me to a steel band practice tonight. Hopefully I'll be good enough to play in the carnival this summer! Dad's friend Arthur (he's from St Kitts like Dad) is on the committee that's organising it. He says it will be just like a Caribbean carnival. I've never been to one because I was born in Leeds, but Mum says there's nothing better! She's helping sew the costumes – she's brilliant at sewing – she works at Burtons on the sewing machines.

There's going to be a carnival queen, a steel band and a procession starting in Potternewton Park.

The procession's going to end up at the Town Hall where there's going to be dancing and a steel band competition. I can't wait!

A police officer enjoys the Leeds Carnival in 1975.

Leeds Festival, held on August Bank Holiday, is one of the largest music festivals in the UK.

Leeds United beat Arsenal 1-0 to win the FA Cup in 1972.

Quarry Hill flats, built in 1938, replaced slums. They were an experiment in high-rise living but were demolished just 40 years later.

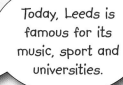
Today, Leeds is famous for its music, sport and universities.

A bomb demolished half of this semi-detached house in Cliff Side Gardens.

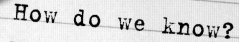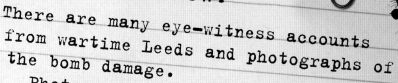

How do we know?

There are many eye-witness accounts from wartime Leeds and photographs of the bomb damage.

Photographs from the 1950s and TV programmes made in Leeds Studios from 1968 show us what life was like in Leeds at that time. Leeds was prosperous. There are recollections of trips with the Leeds coach company Wallace Arnold Tours Ltd. Family snapshots survive of holidays at popular seaside resorts such as Filey. From the 1970s, wealthier people began to take package holidays abroad, flying from Leeds Bradford Airport.

CELT 500 BC	ROMAN AD 43-410	ANGLO-SAXON AD 450-1066	VIKING AD 865-1066	MEDIEVAL TIMES 1066-1485

Leeds Today and Tomorrow

Leeds' history can be discovered and enjoyed in lots of ways. You can see and touch objects at the Leeds City Museum, visit Armley Mills, walk up Briggate and shop in Kirkgate Market. The important thing to remember is that Leeds' history is about the people who lived through difficult or exciting or dangerous times – people like Ruth, John, Tom, Alice, Rose and Lester!

Leeds TV Studios were the first colour studios in Europe when they opened in 1968.

At the Royal Armouries in Clarence Dock you can find out about the history of warfare including jousting, armour and cannons.

The 'Dalek' in Bridgewater Place is the tallest building in Leeds.

Temple Newsam is an Elizabethan country house built over 500 years ago. Today it is open to the public. Will it still be here in another 500 years?

Once, Leeds Waterfront was a bustling industrial highway. Today, it hosts the Leeds Waterfront Festival featuring music dance and...boats!

...1934 ALAN BENNETT BORN...1963 FIRST LEEDS INTERNATIONAL PIANO COMPETITION...

You should feel proud to be a part of Leeds' future.

Headingley Carnegie Stadium is home to Yorkshire County Cricket Club, Leeds Rhinos and Leeds Carnegie.

Leeds United Football Club have played at Elland Road since they formed in 1919.

Leeds University began as a school of medicine. Today it offers a whole range of courses.

'The Rusty Building' was completed in 2010. Will modern buildings like this still be around in 100 years' time?

Kirkgate Market is as popular with shoppers today as it was in Victorian times.

How will they know?

Will Leeds always look like it does now? How will future generations know what Leeds was like today? The Internet is a great way of recording what Leeds is like today. Photos, blogs and stories from tourists can all spread the word about our wonderful Leeds. Or maybe you'll be famous one day and put Leeds on the map!

Glossary

Abbey – a Christian monastery or convent, run by an abbott.

AD – a short way of writing the Latin words anno Domini, which mean 'in the year of our Lord', i.e. after the birth of Christ.

Barge – a flat-bottomed boat for carrying heavy loads, especially on canals.

BC – a short way of writing 'before the birth of Christ'.

Bodkin – a blunt needle for threading ribbon or cord.

Cholera – a deadly disease caused by filthy water.

Cistercian monks – a Roman Catholic religious order of monks.

Clogs – wooden shoes.

Clothier – a person who makes or sells cloth or clothing.

Domesday Book – William the Conqueror sent his men all over England to record the land and wealth in the kingdom, and who owned it. The results of this survey were written in the Domesday Book.

Evacuate – leaving your home quickly to live somewhere safe.

Fleece – the wool from a sheep.

Fulling – a stage in woollen cloth-making which involves the cleansing of cloth to get rid of oils and dirt, and making it thicker.

Haggle – to argue about a price and come to an agreement.

Hand loom – a device used to weave cloth, powered by hand.

Latin – a language originally spoken in Ancient Rome.

Manor – the landed estate of a lord (including the house on it).

Medieval – another term for the Middle Ages.

Merchant – a person who buys and sells goods in order to make a living.

Middle Ages – a period of time roughly from AD 1000 to the 15th century.

Monk – a male member of a religious community.

Munitions – weapons and explosives.

Plague (Black Death) – a serious disease that is carried by rats and can be transferred to humans by fleas.

Privy – a room or building with a toilet inside.

Roundhead – anyone who fought on the side of Parliament against Charles I in the English Civil War.

Royal Charter – written permission from the king or queen to do something.

Royalist – anyone who fought on the side of Charles I in the English Civil War.

Shuttle – a metal-tipped piece of wood that carries the weaving thread at speed from one side of the cloth to the other.

Slums – rundown housing areas where people are very poor.

Ventilation – providing a flow of fresh air.

Wattle and daub – a method of building houses using sticks covered in mud and animal dung.

Workhouse – a large public building where poor people could live as a last resort in exchange for work.

Index

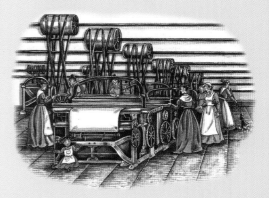

Acknowledgements

The author and publishers would like to thank the following people for their generous help:
Rose Gibson of Leodis for images

The publishers would like to thank the following people and organizations
for their permission to reproduce material on the following pages:
p5: Leeds Museum and Galleries (City Art Gallery); p8: By kind permission of Leeds Library and Information Services,
www.leodis.net; p12: By kind permission of Leeds Library and Information Services, www.leodis.net;
p15: By kind permission of Leeds Library and Information Services, www.leodis.net;
p17: Hartley Greens Leeds Pottery-www.leedspottery.co.uk; p19: Illustrated London News Ltd/Mary Evans;
p21: Bath in Time; p22: By kind permission of Leeds Library and Information Services, www.leodis.net;
p23: Carlsberg; p24: By kind permission of Leeds Library and Information Services, www.leodis.net;
p26: The Guardian/Alamy; p27: By kind permission of Leeds Library and Information Services, www.leodis.net,
Fox Photos / Hulton Archive / Getty Images;
p29: Billy_Bremner_statue-e-www.flickr.com/photos/chrisrobertshaw/2598471903/Wikipedia

All other images copyright of Hometown World Ltd

Every effort has been made to trace and acknowledge the ownership of copyright.
If any rights have been omitted, the publishers offer to rectify this in any future editions.

Written by Gillian Rogerson
Educational consultant: Neil Thompson
Local history consultants: Katherine Baxter and Kitty Ross
Designed by Jemma Cox

Illustrated by Kate Davies, Dynamo Ltd, Virginia Gray, Peter Kent, John McGregor,
Leighton Noyes, Nick Shewring and Tim Sutcliffe
Additional photographs by Alex Long

First published by HOMETOWN WORLD in 2011
Hometown World Ltd
7 Northumberland Buildings
Bath BA1 2JB

www.hometownworld.co.uk

Copyright © Hometown World Ltd 2011

ISBN 978-1-84993-003-1

Your past
Your now
Your future

Your history4ever

Mmm... Still love chocolate pudding!

My next one's going to have 2 wheels!

Trophy for the trendiest glasses?

I love you too!